Tony

# I Wish
## Someone Had Told Me That

# I Wish

**Ten Kernels of Experience
For Those Beginning Their Careers
From Those Concluding Theirs**

**Tony Altilia**

Foreword by
**Dr. Alan Middleton**

Someone
Had Told Me
That

books

Published in 2008 by
**BPS Books**
Toronto, Canada
www.bpsbooks.net
A division of Bastian Publishing Services Ltd.

ISBN 978-0-9809231-7-9

Cataloguing-in-Publication Data
available from Library and Archives Canada.

Design: Malcolm Waddell
Cover and text illustrations: Dominic Buggato

To my sons,
**Zachary, Elliott, and Jason,**
who have taught me
that anything is possible

# Contents

# Foreword

# 10%

As a good marketing person Tony promises ten lessons but actually delivers eleven. (A ten percent bonus!)

Many of the lessons, such as "Dream Big," "Stay on the Learning Curve," and "Put People First," have been discussed in other works. Tony has provided a great service, however, by putting them and others between two covers. And he does so with an appealing freshness, frankness, and approachability. As such, these lessons provide value not only to those starting their careers but to those at any stage of their career.

But there is an eleventh value: the value of reflection. One of the characteristics of great leaders is the ability to reflect, review, and learn. The stories Tony tells of his journey with his friends and colleagues throughout his career are a powerful lesson in the value of reflection — a lesson others can follow by making connections with their own experiences, however long or short.

Enjoy the journey, apply the principles, and reflect. It will be worth it.

**Dr. Alan Middleton**
*Schulich School of Business*
York University
Toronto, Canada

Acknowledgm

**W**hen I shared the idea of
this book with friends and colleagues, they
encouraged me to pursue it and gladly
contributed their own advice. At times it
felt as if they were writing the book and
I was just providing the pen. I owe them
my gratitude.

I also owe a special thanks to Don Bastian,
who not only was my writing tutor but
also is my agent and publisher.

And to my wife, Jo, who encouraged me—
at this juncture, as at so many previous
ones—to dream big.

**Tony Altilia**

# Introduction

**H**aving retired from corporate life at fifty-seven, I soon realized that with retirement comes freedom and free time.

I had the time to do things I had neglected for decades and the freedom to do them on my own terms.

I had more time to spend now with my adult sons and my wife.

I had time to reconnect with old friends.

I had time to manage my finances.

I even had time to organize my sock drawer.

And I had time to think back on my career and my life—on what I had accomplished and what I had learned.

These reflections led to three observations, which in turn led to the writing of this book.

The first was that I had learned a great deal about life, leadership, people, and business during my career. I knew a lot more at the end of my career than I did at the beginning.

The second was that the same was true of my "fellow travelers." During the thirty-three years that I worked for major multinational advertising agencies in Canada and the United States, I traveled the globe for business and pleasure. I was exposed at home and abroad to a number of different cultures and businesses and met a multitude of bright people. I knew that they too had learned a great deal over the course of their careers.

And the third was that all this knowledge and experience needed to be handed over to those who could benefit from it most: young people who are starting their careers just as we are abandoning ours.

I was perhaps particularly motivated to write this book by my three sons. All are of the Millennium Generation and about to venture into their own careers. I knew they would be more likely to read what I had to say than listen to me pontificating about it over Sunday dinner.

So I approached forty-nine colleagues and friends with an average of thirty years' experience each—a combined 1,470 years—and asked them to share their knowledge and wisdom.

The contributors come from all walks of life, including business, health care, not-for-profit, education, and sports.

What follows are ten important career and life lessons—ten kernels of experience—that I, and they, wish we had known when we were starting our careers three decades ago. We may or may not have been more successful if we had been armed with this knowledge then, but we certainly would have been much better prepared for the challenges that lay ahead of us.

My hope—our hope—is to save you some time as you enter into the challenging and enjoyable years of your career.

1

BIG

Dream

**W**hile my agency was working on an advertising campaign for the United Way of Greater Toronto, we interviewed a Somali refugee.

The campaign featured people the United Way had helped to overcome adversity. Unlike previous campaigns, it focused on people's hopefulness, not their hopelessness.

Our Somali was a tall, soft-spoken man with a kind smile. The fact that he could smile at all was a major accomplishment.

He had witnessed the slaughter of his parents as a young boy hiding beneath his bed. Fleeing his country's genocide, he immigrated to Canada and, with the help of the United Way, became a successful entrepreneur, the owner of his own computer software business. He was an inspiration.

During the interview, he shared a piece of advice that his father had passed along to him:

**"Dream big dreams; small dreams have no magic."**

Dream big dreams; small dreams have no magic. It's simple. It's powerful.

His father had taught him that anything is possible, absolutely anything, even starting a successful software company in a foreign country.

His father taught him to never give up—to never feel defeated.

Leo Burnett, who against all odds founded an advertising agency in Chicago during the Great Depression, captured the same thought when he said: **"If you reach for the stars, you may not get one, but you won't come up with a handful of mud either."**

The grim economy meant Leo couldn't afford a receptionist, so he put out a bowl of bright red apples to welcome clients. New York was the center of the advertising industry; establishing an agency in Chicago during such desperate times stirred much doubt. The *Chicago Tribune* wrote, "Anyone who starts an advertising agency in Chicago during these times will soon be eating those red apples."

Leo's agency grew to be one of the largest advertising agencies in the world. Even today, if you visit any of their offices around the globe, you will be greeted by a bowl of apples ... and now a receptionist, too.

Dream big and anything is possible.

Don't be afraid to dream. Don't be afraid to believe in yourself. Don't underestimate your potential.

> **"I wish I had understood my own potential better. I underestimated what was possible for me and often think that perhaps I didn't aim high enough."**
> John Farrow

I was a shy kid from a lower-middle-income family, the grandson of an immigrant Italian cobbler. As if by osmosis, most of my friends and family absorbed the ability to work from our parents and immigrant forefathers.

My grandfather worked hard and raised eleven children on a shoemaker's wage. My dad followed him as a small business entrepreneur and there were five of us.

Working hard was passed from generation to generation, but we lacked the confidence of those who came from more established backgrounds.

My confidence was never more shaken than after my first year of high school. I hadn't been academically inclined during that year, putting my time and energy into pursuing sports, a class captaincy, and a cute cheerleader (whom I eventually married).

As a result, my marks were lousy. I was given the choice of repeating grade nine, going to summer school, or (as the guidance counselor strongly encouraged me) attending the four- versus five-year matriculation program, because "some people aren't smart enough to go to university." The five-year program was a prerequisite for attending university.

The government had just started a community college system and was encouraging students—including those from the four-year high-school stream—to attend. This was the option I chose.

I enjoyed the community college experience and while attending won an academic bursary in marketing. I went on after graduation to attend a university business school if for no other reason than to prove my guidance counselor wrong.

My confidence had been shaken but not stirred. I did graduate with an honors business degree, from Wilfrid Laurier University. My only regret is not sharing my degree with that misguided counselor. It might have prompted him to encourage his subsequent tutelages to dream big, to reach for the stars.

**"Be confident in your ability to be an independent thinker. Don't be intimidated by people who out-talk you."**
Henry Fiorillo

Dream Big. Choose a career you love and pursue it. If you love music, pursue a music career. If you love gardening, pursue a life of gardening.

Part of my career was spent in Chicago. While there we were always impressed by how happy my son Elliott's guitar teacher was. Dave worked in a music store, taught children how to play guitar, and played in a rock band. He loved what he did. You could see it. You could feel it.

Do something you like, not something your folks or your friends like. Follow your heart as well as your head to find your true passion.

My love of marketing and advertising began in college. A guest speaker, John Anderson, who was then a young account executive, told us about his job. He loved it. He loved its diversity, its pace, and its people. John turned me on to the industry. And almost by fate, he would become my client ten years later.

Advertising combined business, human behavior, and art—all subjects that I was inherently interested in. I was fascinated by the challenge of understanding how and why consumers made choices—and how through the combination of smart problem solving and art one could influence those choices.

No, I didn't wake up one day and suddenly realize I wanted to work for an advertising agency, but I did follow my heart and my instincts and over time discovered a career I loved.

**"I wish I had totally understood what Leo meant by his most famous quote. I now know it meant to set ambitious goals—dream big—but to not just stick them in a drawer. To re-examine them often, assess your progress, and make new plans to continue your journey to the stars."**
Jim McKenzie

Jo and I got married between my second and third year of university. While she taught school, we lived the poor student life. We struggled to pays the bills, often taking advances on our VISA credit card to make payments on our Shell gas card; Jo was our only source of income and she needed the car to get to work in a neighboring town.

We lived paycheck to paycheck. Many Sunday mornings we robbed the penny jar to treat ourselves to a Tim Hortons coffee and apple fritter in an attempt to assuage the pains of a well-deserved hangover. That was our extravagant treat for the week.

The advertising business pays well and it provided our family a comfortable life. And yes, money is important, but many Boomers have learned—some of us the hard way—that money is a byproduct of success, not success in and of itself.

**"Don't always go for the money. Pick jobs that excite you over jobs that don't but pay more. You will be more likely to excel when you are doing what you love. The money will come as a consequence."**
Trevor Collier

Success is defined by more than money. Those who inspired me most throughout my career had a multitude of interests outside work and beyond accumulating wealth. They accumulated knowledge and a wide range of experiences besides the money.

The people I found the most uninteresting and the most boring were those who believed that money was a yardstick of success. I never really cared what kind of a car someone drove or how many watches and homes they owned. I wasn't interested in whether someone preferred wearing Gucci or Rockport shoes.

**"Do what you love and don't settle for less. I wish I'd worked harder at finding what I loved to do versus what I was good at."**
Daryl Elliott

Your dreams will change with time. They will evolve in concert with your experiences.

I was recruited from university by the Campbell Soup Company to work in their marketing department. I thought it was the perfect job for me, given that I had majored in marketing. I loved it.

Initially.

It *was* the ideal place for me to apply my academic learning. I was, albeit at the most junior level, involved in product formulation, new product development, packaging, sales promotion, pricing, consumer behavior, and advertising—all of which I had just studied at business school.

I soon realized, however, that I liked the advertising part of my job the most. I loved going to the company's advertising agency, Ogilvy & Mather, and talking about the strategy and the creative expression of the strategy. I really loved the people. They were diverse, interested in many things, irreverent, and far less formal than we were at Campbell's.

Early in my career, my dream was changing. I wanted to work for an ad agency rather than as a client. I left Campbell after two and a half years, moved to an agency, and stayed in the advertising industry for thirty years.

I worked for three multinational advertising agencies in three great cities, Toronto, Montreal, and Chicago. I worked across every conceivable business, from fast food to slow gin. I embraced change. It fueled me. It kept me fresh. It kept me engaged. It energized me. Perhaps I suffer from ADD, but I love the challenge of change.

Unlike the generations who preceded us, many of us Boomers have had many jobs and many careers. And that doesn't look to be changing anytime soon for those of you starting your careers today.

**"You will have many careers in your lifetime. Your last job will likely be in a different industry and utilize a skill set you do not have today; maybe in a field not yet invented."**
Mary Colleen Shanahan

Embrace change. Don't shy away from it. If anything is constant in life, it is change.

**"At the time I graduated from Wharton with my MBA, in 1976, I felt it would be boring to work in a financial institution and much preferred the notion of working in an operating company where one was involved in providing tangible products. Now that I have spent nine years in private equity and have been exposed to a wide variety of financial institutions, I feel my assumption was incorrect."**
Robert Hall

## KERNEL OF EXPERIENCE

Dream big dreams; small dreams have no magic.

Follow your heart as well as your head.

Take the time to assess what you love and do your best to build a career around it.

Dream

# 2

# Work

ard

**W**ork is a four-letter word, but it's not a dirty word.

Boomers, many of whom marched in protest against "the man" in the 1960s, today say that their success is the result of hard work. In the 1960s, however, hard work was a value they would have ascribed to their parents, not themselves. It was a value they were protesting against.

That was not as true for me.

As mentioned above, I picked up the power of hard work from my parents, but as a teenager I lacked the confidence of others.

My father, the son of an immigrant cobbler, and the tenth of eleven children, grew up in a tiny row house in Toronto's Little Italy. While he may have lost a few inches in his elderly years, he was always a bear of a man, big and strong on the outside, soft on the inside.

A child of the Depression, he attended Toronto's Central Technical High School, eventually becoming a tool and die maker, a trade he practiced early in his career. University wasn't an option for many Depression or immigrant children, including him.

In 1961, by then the father of five children, Dad started a small welding equipment repair business with two of his brothers. He worked long hard hours, often logging eleven hours a day, six and seven days a week.

I often felt stress in my career, but not that kind of stress. Owning your own company, eating what you kill, and making payroll while supporting a family is much more stressful than any job I ever had.

He once told me, "We started the business when your younger brother, John, was born. I came home one night and he was eleven."

My mother, concerned that we would grow up not knowing our dad, encouraged him to take us to work with him on Saturdays. We swept the shop floor and cleaned the lunchroom and bathrooms.

Once I reached my teenage years, I spent summers working alongside him in the plant. I tried to match his hours, often coming up short.

While I wouldn't have said so at the time, I was learning the power of hard work. I was learning to be unafraid of work.

**"Good enough never is. Your success in life will be a result of taking the extra few minutes to finish the last mile."**
Ginny Dybenko

Those of you among today's twenty-somethings—variously called the Millennium Generation or Generation Y—do have a different set of expectations from the generations who preceded you: the Baby Boomers and the Gen Xers.

Bruce Tulgran, founder of the leading generational-research firm Rainmaker Thinking, says this about Gen Yers in an article in *Fortune Magazine* (May 28, 2007):

"This is the most high-mainte-nance workforce in the history of the world. The good news is they're going to be the most high-performing workforce in the history of the world. They walk in with more informa-tion in their heads, more information at their fingertips. Sure, they have high expectations, but they have the highest expectations first and foremost for themselves."

He adds: "While Gen Yers will work a 60-hour week if they have to—and might even do so happily if they're paid enough to make the most of their precious downtime—they don't want that to be in the way of life."

> **"Applied effort is just as important as a good idea."**
>
> John Farrow

I spent thirty of my thirty-three-year career working for advertising agencies. They attract an eclectic array of people who share a common trait: They're all pretty darn smart.

I was never the smartest, but my competitive instincts ensured I was always one of the hardest workers, especially in my early years. If I had been an athlete, I would have been a grinder: not the most skilled player on the team but one of the hardest working. I just put my head down and got things done.

Young advertising people, like young lawyers, accountants, and doctors, log long hours. It's part of their apprenticeship in a professional-services company.

Tony Houghton, the chairman of Leo Burnett, Canada, addressed an overworked staff in a company meeting in the late 1980s by saying, "If you want regular hours, a guaranteed pension, and every day that is much the same, join the Post Office. But if you love change and challenge and interesting people, work in an ad agency."

**"There's no replacing hard work.
No matter how smart you are, if you don't
put in the extra effort, you won't go very far."**
Casey Forrest

**"Thinking is hard work.
Knowledge is not enough; applying it is
the trick."**
Laurence Berstein

You'll begrudge working hard
if you don't like your job. I was unhappiest
when I traveled excessively on business.
I didn't like being separated from my young
family.

Traveling is hard work. In fact,
it's more stressful to travel around the world
alone than to deal with tough clients, staff, or
creative issues at home.

On one occasion I flew from
Chicago overnight to London, showered in
the first-class lounge, met a colleague, flew
to Nice, France, for a two-hour meeting, and
then flew back to London. The following day
I was off to Asia and visited seven countries
in nine days, before returning to Chicago.
Thirty-six hours later, I flew to South America
and visited three countries in six days. By
the time I finally got home I didn't know what
city or time zone I was in.

**"Work hard on new things. Being smart or even skilled is a real advantage, but working hard on doing good work and being willing to take on new challenges may be even more valuable."**
Tom Collinger

I didn't really appreciate the value of people willing to give a little extra until I led a department and then a company.

As an agency CEO, I grew to rely most on the people who took it on themselves to go beyond the expected, to work a little harder. The ones who asked for forgiveness rather than permission. These were the ones who got noticed. The ones who were given more responsibility and authority. These were the go-to people.

**"If you want something done, give it to a busy person."**
Eric Larson

During the late 1970s and early 1980s, the Canadian economy suffered from high interest rates, inflation, and a general malaise. Marketing and advertising budgets and consequently advertising jobs were the first to be cut during these tough economic times. Hundreds of marketing and advertising executives lost their jobs in Toronto, thousands in New York.

19

I had just bought a house and my wife and I were planning a family, which we agreed would take us down to one income. We were swimming in debt, so losing my job was not an option.

Job security meant making myself indispensable to my clients and my employer. I survived while others failed. I kept my job and got promoted while the streets were flooded with unemployed ad execs. I may not have been as talented as others, but I was more committed and thus was less dispensable.

**"No matter what anybody tells you, during layoffs the keepers get to stay. To be a keeper you have to bring special value. Sometimes it's the really smart people or the creative people who think of ways to generate this value. Sometimes working hard can generate this value. Always ask yourself, 'What am I doing to differentiate myself in a big way?'"**

Art Horn

Activity should not be confused with working smart, however. Being busy and being productive are not the same. I have to admit I often worked and kept busy just to demonstrate that I could do it. I often wrote unnecessary market analyses and competitive reviews to impress my boss and my clients.

Few if any of these initiatives resulted in more business for the client or the agency. I could recite market share, distribution, and pricing data for my brands and those of the competitors, but on reflection, I'm not sure any of this helped move the business forward or accomplished much.

**"I learned to focus on accomplishments, not activity. Delivering your project list doesn't matter; what truly matters is getting things done, accomplishing things. Having a passion for making a difference is contagious. It starts at the most junior level."**
Greg Shearson

Work will be more fun if you find an organization that focuses on results rather than working for work's sake.

I was the least happy at Leo
Burnett, Chicago. When I was there, the
company was consumed with internal politics.
There was little laughter in meetings. It was
joyless. And the results were lousy. They lost
a lot more business than they won during my
five years there.

I was happiest at Leo Burnett,
Toronto. Same company, different culture. I
felt the most comfortable there, the most at
home. It was collegial. It was fun. Meetings
were filled with laughter. The firm was committed to doing great work for all of its clients.
I worked there from 1988 to 1993, and many
of the folks I met then continue to be my close
friends today. And our results were great. We
doubled the size of the agency in five years.

> **"Work in a company that
> has the same values as you, values that you
> truly believe in."**
> Ted Clarke

> **"Values and organization
> cultures vary. Do your homework. Align your
> values with your company's, and if they do
> not match, move."**
> Bob Millar

## KERNEL OF
## EXPERIENCE

In most professions you'll be
required to work hard.

Work on those things that will
ultimately make a difference.

Don't confuse activity with
accomplishment.

Work in a company with the same
values as yours.

# 3

# Master the Balance Bea

**M**arcus Aurelius said, **"Live each act as if it were your last."**

Maintaining the proper work–life balance was an important lesson that many of us Boomers wish we'd learned early in our careers. This may seem to contradict the "work hard" lesson, but it doesn't.

Boomers often worked for the sake of working. We often confused activity with productivity. We manufactured work to appear busy.

You Millennials can teach us Boomers a few lessons about work–life balance. You don't mind working hard; you just want to know why. You want to know the end-game. You want to know what's in it for you. Most of us Boomers weren't that smart.

Many of us forfeited vacations, weekends, and family time to pursue work and careers. Many moved our families from city to city or country to country in pursuit of the next promotion.

I started my career as an assistant brand manager for the Campbell Soup Company, working on the not-so-high-flying brands of Franco-American Canned Pasta and Swanson TV Dinners. My career almost lasted longer than these brands.

I was twenty-four years old and regularly worked eighty-hour weeks, often eating all three meals in the company cafeteria.

My dad had done it standing on his feet most of the day. Surely I could do it sitting at a desk—and besides, cheap soup can be a great motivator to a newly minted 1974 business graduate making $9,000 a year.

My colleagues worked just as hard and just as long because it was expected. To this day, I don't fully understand why, other than that it was a badge of courage or resilience.

Our courage and resilience were tested often. Some of us survived the test and the autocracy, but others left to pursue other less-time-demanding jobs and to dream big in other professions. Companies lost smart, productive people who would have been capable of making profitable contributions, had the environments been more caring.

I was also driven by fear.

One of my first assignments was to manage the production of 35 mm slides for the national sales meeting. I was given a month to complete the task.

It was a big deal. Bobby Hull, the ex-NHL superstar, was the motivational speaker. Senior executives from both the Canadian and American companies would be attending. There was no greater opportunity to mess up than at this meeting.

There was no PowerPoint in 1974. Presentations were created and shot on 35 mm film, developed into slides, and shown on a projector. The lead-time was weeks, not minutes.

Campbell had enlisted an event-planning company, which in turn recommended a graphic designer we had never used before. His studio was located halfway between our offices and my home. Driven by paranoia and an intuitive distrust of this man, I checked in with him three times a week on my way home from work. He never had anything to show me—nothing, ever.

His constant reply was, "Don't worry. I'll get it done." His reassurances only heightened my suspicions. With only a week left before the meeting and still no slides, I shared my fear with the marketing VP. He encouraged me not to fret. "The designer is a creative person," he said. "It's just the nature of the beast."

We were scheduled to present on a Sunday, with rehearsals starting on Saturday. Thursday night I picked up the rolls of film from the studio and took them to an overnight film developer. At sunrise, after a night of tossing and turning and a bad case of the cold sweats, I picked the slides up and rushed them to the office. I nervously put them in a projector and showed them to my boss.

They were awful. Unreadable.

My stomach turned as I visualized an early ending to a very short career. My first solo project and it was an utter mess.

It looked as if I was doomed to be sweeping my dad's shop floor forever.

The VP of marketing called Ogilvy & Mather, our advertising agency. They had just discovered a method of creating computer-generated slides, so we rushed to their offices and spent the day recreating the material. O&M saved a few careers that weekend, mine included.

My life was totally out of balance for that month and several other times throughout my career. I lost perspective in the middle of all the stress.

**"No one is indispensable. J.L. Kraft, the founder of Kraft, once said, 'Show me an indispensable employee and I will fire him because no one should be that important to an organization.' Remember that when you think of work–life balance. I gave up vacation time early in my career, much to my ultimate chagrin."**
Bob Millar

Losing balance and perspective also takes its toll on families.

I moved my family from Toronto to Montreal back to Toronto then to Chicago and back again to Toronto because of my job and my career. No one made me do it. I wanted it. It fueled my ego. I was chosen over others. I was advancing my career.

Each and every move was a great adventure and a learning experience for our family, but my wife, Jo, and our three sons made many more sacrifices than I did.

I would move to the new job and city and leave Jo to deal with the real estate agents, the movers, and the children. Once she joined me, she was pretty much left on her own to find a house, schools, doctors, and often me.

And it was easier for me to meet people because I was working. Jo was stuck driving the boys from one event to another with little time to make new friends. Moving is lonely for spouses.

We moved to Chicago on New Year's Eve 1994 and spent the night in a rented apartment overlooking Lake Michigan's frozen shores, questioning why we had left the comfortable confines of Toronto. A new city with no extended family nearby and no house is exciting and frightening at one and the same time.

I asked my second son, Elliott, when he was twenty-two, about the effect of these multiple moves on him and our relationship. I asked him in particular how he felt about me during the five years we spent in Chicago.

While not meant to be, his response was a "heart punch." Without any malice, he simply said, "Dad, I don't remember you in Chicago. I remember you coming to my hockey games and being home at Christmas, but otherwise I don't remember you being there."

And he's right. I wasn't there. I wasn't there physically because of the travel and long work hours. I wasn't there emotionally because when I was home I was too exhausted to be fully engaged with him or anyone else in my family.

Yes, you'll have to work hard, but make time for yourself, your friends, and your family. Play as hard as you work. Have fun.

**"Family first. Balance is integral to success. If your identity is tied to what you do as opposed to who you are, you won't be a sound decision maker."**
Bernie Dyer

Laugh out loud every day and treat each one as it was the last day of the rest of your life.

Have as much passion for life as for work.

**"If it isn't fun and you can't make it so, find something or some place that is."**
Tim McChesney

Learn to master the balance beam. Don't be afraid to work hard, but not just for the sake of working hard.

**"I wish I had found a more reasonable balance with my work life and what I gave up on the personal and family side."**
Bruce Elliott

**"Have fun. Don't take yourself too seriously. We're not talking about life and death here."**
Terry Jackson

Unlike us Boomers, who worked for work's sake, who worked to impress our bosses with dogged determination, you have a healthier perspective on work and how it fits into your life.

You are more inclined to work to live as opposed to Boomers who lived to work. You seek employers that promote work–life balance. You view your time away from work as precious and will do almost anything to protect it.

You seek employers that provide you with constant and new challenges and with the flexibility to pursue a life outside of work.

**"Don't take yourself too seriously; have some fun along the way."**
Pauleen Home

I worked for Alan Middleton during the early 1980s. Alan is now a business professor at York University. When we worked together he was the president of Enterprise Advertising, a small agency owned by J. Walter Thompson.

Alan was a self-confessed workaholic, regularly logging eighty-hour workweeks.

Try as I might, I just couldn't outwork him.

Often I would arrive at the parking garage at 7 a.m. and sneak over to touch the hood of his Mustang. It was usually cool, leading me to conclude that he had stayed at the office all night.

We lovingly nicknamed him "Thank God it's Monday Middleton" and teased him that his favorite saying was, "If you don't come in on Saturday, don't bother coming in on Sunday."

Even Alan wishes he had done a better job of mastering the balance beam.

**"I wish I had understood the importance of vacations."**
Alan Middleton

Another of my bosses, Frank Palmer, chairman of DDB Group Canada and the industry's most skillful practical joker, echoes many Boomers' thoughts.

**"Most of what I did early in my career didn't matter. Early in my career, so much of what I got excited about or anxious about or wasted time and energy on, turned out not to matter. There are really only a few things that truly count for a happy and successful life. I wish I had known better to concentrate on those and not waste my time on the rest."**
Frank Palmer

## KERNEL OF
## EXPERIENCE

- Laugh out loud every day.

- Remember what is truly important in life.

- Follow Stonewall Jackson's advice: "Never take counsel of your fears."

Master the Balance Beam

# 4

# Embrace a GOD Father

When I look back over my career, I'm embarrassed to recall what a jerk I was early on. I had graduated from business school, was recruited by a packaged goods company, and like all other biz school grads was determined to be the company president in two years.

I cringe at the thought of it now.

**"Be humble. Don't be too arrogant. I was a bit cocky early in my career."**
Terry Jackson

I figured I could go it alone. I could master any challenge. I naively believed I didn't need the advice and counsel of others. I didn't need a Godfather. I didn't need a mentor.

How wrong I was.

If I had been smarter, if I had known then what I know now, I would have made a concerted effort within the first year of my career to find the smartest person I could and ask him or her to become my trusted advisor.

Mentors don't have to be people you work with or for. They should be someone you admire, someone you respect, someone with the knowledge and experience you don't yet have.

**"Mentors are all around you.
Be open to learn from everyone you meet,
work, and play with."**
Jo Altilia

Over time—in hindsight, too much time—I came to understand the importance of seeking the advice, wisdom, and counsel of people I liked and respected.

I had several over the course of my career.

One was a fellow by the name of Paul Edgar. Paul was a big man—close to six three and larger than life. He wasn't the smoothest of characters, but he was a lovable beast who had won the respect and admiration of the agency's creative department. They trusted him. They liked him because he worked at being their friend and because he helped them hone their work, supporting it and selling it to our clients. He never ever bailed on them or their work.

I worked for Paul when I left Campbell Soup and moved to the agency side. I knew nothing about encouraging great advertising from creative teams. I acted the same way I had as a client. My view was that as long as I wrote the brief and managed the client, it was up to the creative teams to deliver the work, with little interaction from me. If we sold it, great. If not, it was their responsibility, not mine.

Early on, Paul took me aside and tutored me in how to work with creative teams. He made it clear how difficult my life would be if they didn't like or respect me. He showed me how to build trust with them. He taught me that simply demanding great work wasn't enough.

Paul mentored me in the art of collaboration. He encouraged me to socialize with the creative folks outside of work, to get to know them as people and not just associates.

Paul was instrumental in kick-starting my agency life.

**"Seek advice widely, from parents, family, friends, mentors, and colleagues. Evaluate it carefully, and then make decisions that are your own. You never need to feel alone. You are surrounded by other people who have had thoughts, problems, and experiences similar to your own."**
Dr. David Ouchterlony

By far my most influential mentor was Tony Houghton. Tony is a Brit who graduated from Cambridge, taught mathematics, wrote comedy for Peter Sellers, and worked directly with David Ogilvy. Tony and I first met when I was a young Campbell client and he was the creative director of Olgilvy & Mather Toronto.

Tony also helped recruit me to Burnett when he was the chairman of Leo Burnett, Canada. I learned a lot from him. He taught me that being liked is just as important as being respected. He taught me how to recognize and encourage great creative ideas. He taught me that a dry wit and a keen sense of humor are valuable tools in business and in life. They help ease the tension in tough situations. He even taught me the fine art of the two-martini lunch, an art that is thankfully on the wane today.

I didn't plan to have Tony as a mentor. It happened by circumstance. We had met when I was his client, and even in those early days he looked out for me. On several occasions he counseled me in the craft of creative evaluation.

Seek out a mentor. It doesn't have to be your boss or even someone you work with. In fact it probably shouldn't be. The advice will be more honest.

**"I initially thought that my mentor was my immediate boss. In many cases this will be as far away from a mentor as you can get. Seek mentors inside and outside your company. Choose those who can give you sage advice and from whom you can learn. They will help you navigate the often choppy waters of the corporate world. Many of them will develop into lifelong colleagues."**
Jim McKenzie

Choose a mentor you like, respect, and trust. Your mentor must possess all three characteristics. Simply liking and respecting a mentor is not enough. A strong mentor relationship is built on trust. You must trust them and they must trust you.

I had a boss at Leo Burnett, Chicago who gave me a remarkable piece of advice.

I had just finished a very disturbing conversation with a client who had lied to me, and unabashedly so. I was frustrated and upset and sought out my boss's advice if for no other reason than to vent or at least share the pain.

I told him the client had barefaced lied to me and I didn't trust or like him or his company. My boss's reply was simple: "Tony, you can't trust anyone."

I thought this odd advice coming from someone I worked for. Was he telling me not to trust him, too?

Strong bonding relationships like mentoring ones are built on trust.

Choose your trusted advisor wisely.

**"Model the best. Make every effort necessary to connect with people you really respect. Great people are the ones who become the best teachers, the people from whom you can learn the most. This is likely to be more important than the company where you work, or the work you are there to do."**
Tom Collinger

Many of us Boomers, especially me, didn't make a conscious decision in choosing a mentor. It wasn't planned. Paul and Tony were people I worked with and for. I was lucky that they chose to mentor me. I didn't plan it. I didn't consciously seek anyone out, and I should have.

Seek a mentor. Plan it. Don't leave it to chance.

**"If I had consciously planned my career by identifying specific mentors and the traits I most valued, I would have had a clearer career blueprint. I fell into my mentors and by the time I identified them, several other colleagues had already identified me as their mentor. We are a product of the business leaders who have most touched our careers, but I wish I had been more aware of the profound effect they could have on one's career and life."**
Doug Hayes

We Boomers entered our careers skeptical of anyone over thirty. We were products of the 1960s. We instinctively knew we were the most influential generation of the twentieth century. We influenced everything from music to fashion to politics, not because we were any smarter than preceding generations but because there were more of us.

We often ignored our seniors' knowledge, and many of us came to know this was a mistake.

**"Identify and commit to a mentor. Create a strong and trusting relationship with someone who cares about your success and offers the insight, guidance, and help to manage the minefield of career progression."**
Fred Jaques

Choose your mentors early. Choose them throughout your career. You can have more than one. Confide in them. Seek their counsel and have them trust you as much as you trust them.

**"Two of the people who matter most in my life are my mentors. I sought out mentors at different stages of my career. I wish I'd done it the minute I graduated. My experience has shown me that if you ask for help, you will get it. Respect the mentor relationship and you'll leap frog ahead in your career."**
Elizabeth Mast Priestman

**"In hindsight virtually all the advice and truisms I heard when I was young turned out to be true. So maybe I'd therefore say one thing: I wish I knew then that most of the classic advice given by sage elders was actually worth listening to."**
Michael MacMillan

## KERNEL OF EXPERIENCE

Choose a mentor early in your career.

Make it a considered choice.

Seek out those you like and respect, and trust will follow.

# 5

# Jump IN

**I** remember being slightly in awe of our VP of marketing, Jerry Young, and other senior executives when I was a young brand assistant at Campbell Soup. They all seemed so smart, so polished. Nothing seemed to faze them. They were calm and confident during even the most difficult times. And they had offices to boot. Offices with doors while the rest of us sat in small cubicles, or as Douglas Coupland calls them, "feeding pens."

As I gained more confidence, I realized that the people I admired most in my early years weren't any smarter than those of us inhabiting the pens; they were just more experienced.

There's no need to be intimidated by more experienced people. They put their pants on one leg at a time. They make mistakes and so will you. It's part of learning. That's why pencils have erasers.

Believe in yourself. Be confident, not arrogant. You were recruited over others for your intellect, your motivation, and your interpersonal skills.

You were selected because others believe in you, so you must, too.

Taking risks requires confidence and courage. Jump in.

**"When you're young, you are reluctant to participate because you feel you don't know anything. You believe everyone in the room knows more than you do. You sit at the back of the room just listening. In truth, your opinion matters. Your thoughts are relevant. Dig down and find the confidence. If you speak up in a strong and confident voice, you'll be heard. No idea is a bad idea. You know more than you think."**

Elizabeth Mast Priestman

Campbell Soup was a conservative, autocratic, and intimidating company when I joined it in the mid-1970s. We were mandated to wear suits and ties every day. No sports jackets. No casual Fridays. At the head office in Camden, New Jersey, you couldn't walk the halls without suit jacket and tie on.

It wasn't for the faint of heart. Every meeting, no matter how minor, was an inquisition. We were challenged as a matter of course. We were tested daily.

Most packaged goods companies were like that then. Anyone who participated in a Procter & Gamble annual budget meeting during those times knows what I'm talking about.

We learned the only way to survive, to gain the requisite confidence, was to jump in.

You are being paid for a point of view, so share it.

49

As I gained experience and confidence, I felt more comfortable sharing my opinion in meetings. I believed our work would be better through debate and the occasional argument. I'd rather be toast than milquetoast. If I lost my job because of my opinion, I was either lousy at my job or working in the wrong culture.

**"Learn to recognize and take a chance on opportunities. This is hard because it involves acceptance of the unexpected. The most rewarding jobs, projects, and relationships I ever had seemed to come into my life by chance. Similarly, the things I now regret passing by were ones I didn't see as opportunities at the time. I know now I lacked the courage to be led in another direction."**
Trevor Collier

Most of us are afraid of making a mistake and many of us are frozen by indecision. No one wants to be judged the fool. But you are more likely to be judged foolish if you don't take some risks and jump in.

**"Don't be afraid to make mistakes and take ownership of your work. Man up and admit when you are wrong. Make sure you learn from your mistakes and strive to get better. Telling the truth is very empowering and means you never have to fear failure."**
Casey Forrest

I may have been outspoken, but I was, reluctant to make mistakes early on. I was afraid of looking foolish. In hindsight I wish I had taken greater risks and asked for forgiveness more often than permission.

You will make mistakes. When you do, don't fret. Learn and move on. Many before you have made mistakes and many more will after you.

**"I wish I had known that you get through and survive anything."**
John Clinton

DDB, a multinational advertising agency, calls their operating principles the Four Freedoms:
- Freedom from Chaos
- Freedom to Fail
- Freedom to Be
- Freedom from Fear

I wish I had understood Freedom from Fear earlier. Being fearless liberates you to take risks, jump in, and be an impact player.

**"Be bold. The meek will not inherit the earth. Once you know what you want, go for it."**
Dr. David Ouchterlony

Jump in, but don't sit in the weeds among the water lilies and the frogs. Be courageous. Swim farther out. Have a point of view and share it.

**"If something needs doing, and no one is doing it, don't be afraid to step forward and take the ownership of the task or situation, even if you don't have any experience in or knowledge of the subject matter. In the absence of leadership, leaders will emerge."**
John McLean

The idea of jumping in, taking the initiative, is more important today than when we Boomers started our careers. More than ever, organizations are trying to do more with less, including less people. They reward those who jump in and take risks.

**"Take the initiative. Don't wait for someone to ask you to jump in."**
Tim McChesney

I was too cautious. As one client of mine, a Vietnam War vet who had flown and captained helicopter missions, said to me, "What's the worst that can happen? No one is firing live bullets."

**"Take risks. Calculated risk is much better for your business, the company, and your career than inertia or complacency."**
Ron Fabbro

You'll never get punished for taking the initiative if it's for the betterment of the organization. You will if your motives are selfish or political.

**"Don't be afraid of making a mistake. Always try your best and don't do anything immoral or illegal. All other mistakes can be corrected. You learn from stumbling, just like a toddler."**
Mary Colleen Shanahan

Organizations will reward impact players, folks who make a difference. If you sit on the sidelines waiting to be called into the game, you'll become a perennial bench warmer, not a high-priced starter.

**"Be the expert or go-to guy. Own one small but high-profile project that is not part of your job. Jump in."**
Bob MacNelly

**"Looking back I missed opportunities by being too conservative. The best memories are of the big bold plays more than of the results."**
Mark Drexler

**"Following the status quo won't get you very far in the corporate world."**
Tom Bene

Many of us Boomers wish we had been bolder at the beginning of our careers. We wish we'd been more innovative and less conservative. We wish someone had told us to forge new ways of doing things, new ways of thinking.

**"You will get ahead by implementing bold plans that have the potential to completely transform the way things are done. When I graduated from university, I had the impression that companies were made up of stodgy, conservative people at the top and energetic mavericks at the bottom. Over time I came to appreciate that people get to the top by thinking out of the box and implementing**

**bold plans that have a dramatic impact on the way things are done. In hindsight, I think I was too conservative early in my career."**
Tim Penner

So don't wait to be asked to do something.

At the same time, however, don't confuse confidence with arrogance.

Creative people are often accused of arrogance—but not the talented ones.

The creative talent I grew to respect were those who had the confidence to let their work speak for itself so they wouldn't have to hide behind a mask of arrogance.

These were the people whose ideas energized the agency and the client.

**"Take action and ask for forgiveness later. If you have to make a choice between good judgment and procedure, always favor good judgment."**
John McLean

**"The best thing I could have done early in my career was to admit openly to mistakes and lack of knowledge when appropriate. It truly does empower you and builds respect and increases your learning exponentially."**
Michael Hogg

Jump in. You will jump-start your learning, and your career. Be brave.

## KERNEL OF EXPERIENCE

Believe in yourself.

Be confident, not arrogant.

Take risks.

Be innovative.

# 6

Stay on the Learning

C U R

Graduating from university doesn't signify the end of your education but just the beginning of an endless learning journey.

The need for the constant pursuit of wisdom and skills is a major lesson we Boomers learned.

The changes in technology that have taken place in the past thirty years would have to be the best example.

As a Campbell Soup brand assistant, I made copies on a noisy duplicating machine, received my phone messages on pink slips, returned phone calls on a landline phone, and communicated almost exclusively face-to-face. Any computing that was done was on a mainframe, which had far less computing capacity than today's laptops.

Most of us didn't know how to type. Letters and memos were dictated to secretaries who recorded them in shorthand and typed them on electric typewriters. They used whiteout, a liquid "paint," to correct errors.

There were no mobile phones, no e-mails, no fax machines, no personal computers, and certainly no BlackBerries.

To survive we had to stay current with changing technology. We had to constantly evolve and learn new skills, which is something that becomes increasingly difficult as you take on more responsibility.

**"Stay abreast of technology and all that is new because it will continue to change how business is and will be done."**
Steve Brown

The hungrier you are for learning, knowledge, and wisdom, the more interested you will be in life and the more interesting you'll be. Your chosen profession doesn't matter. People want to associate with engaging and enlightened people. If you're bored, you'll bore others.

**"Continuing education is the most important way to keep up-to-date, and not just academic education but a thirst for knowledge of all kinds."**
Alan Middleton

I wish I'd followed Alan's advice earlier in my career. I've always had an interest in art and painting, and while I dabbled in it during my twenties, I didn't pursue it with any vigor until my fifties. It took me most of my life to gain the confidence (and the ability to ignore the good-humored ridicule of my pals) to follow this deep-rooted interest.

I am now an art student, not an artist. I paint for fun and have a growing appreciation of those whose livelihood comes from selling their work.

My art education has just started. I continue to learn with each and every lesson and with each and every painting. It's a little scary, but invigorating and exciting at the same time. I am meeting new people in new surroundings. I'm now as comfortable in an art studio as in a boardroom.

Learning energizes us.

I spent most of my career working in advertising agencies and learned that the best agency people are those with a keen and varied interest in the world around them. Advertising is a reflection of society, so staying current in music, film, entertainment, the arts, and politics is essential. The learning curve never stops. It's exponential.

**"I wish I had been on the front end of the technology curve. My career spanned a computer dead zone. We were too young to just ignore technological change but too old to have been properly trained. Technology will come naturally to the Millennium Generation but it will evolve and unfold at warp speed."**
Doug Hayes

**"I wish I had known how important the new technology was going to become."**
Keith Pelley

Continue to learn. Be in constant pursuit of knowledge and wisdom no matter what your interests are. Focusing myopically on your career and industry is limiting.

I left the client side for an advertising agency because I intuitively knew that I was becoming one-dimensional. I was slowly becoming an expert on frozen dinners and canned pasta but not much else. I was becoming bored and boring. I needed more stimuli and believed that the agency world would offer it.

I loved the analytical aspect of product management, but I felt most alive when I visited the advertising agency. I loved the people. They were a much more diverse group than we were as the client. They were artists, writers, producers, designers, and business people.

They had a richer passion for life and all things different. They loved books, history, music, comedy, art, sports, politics, and weaving a good story over a more than occasional pint of beer. They loved life and embraced new experiences.

**"Don't focus on managing your career. Instead, manage your learning curve. People who focus on managing their careers fixate on job titles, compensation, and charting the fast track to the top. My advice would be to focus instead on maximizing your learning. It will help you chart a more interesting course."**
Tim Penner

Have an insatiable appetite to learn. You not only will be more successful at work, you also will be more successful in life. People are attracted to interesting and interested people. Knowledgeable folk are interesting.

61

My wife, Jo, is a great example of someone who has never stopped learning. She has an insatiable appetite to advance her own education. Her interests are wide and varied. A former teacher, she has studied everything from theosophy and psychology to life drawing and painting to jewelry making and the culinary arts.

She also has the uncanny ability to read four books at the same time without confusing the stories. I get confused if I read the newspaper's sports section before the general news.

Jo's passion for reading and learning helped her create a successful charity that empowers young teen moms through the written word. Her passion became her work. She transforms lives.

Learning doesn't come just from books and courses. Trevor Collier, who has contributed to this book and was a qualitative researcher most of his career, continues to learn by traveling the globe. He and his wife, Sarah, have a great thirst to learn about other cultures and countries, and it is quenched only when they visit and immerse themselves in them. No big hotels. No lazy beach days.

They visited Vietnam when it was migrating from a Communist to a market system. They have traveled extensively through Mexico, and have a scholarly interest in South America, as evidenced by their visits to Peru, Bolivia, and Argentina.

**"Never think you know enough. Be a sponge and learn as much as you can. This will allow you to converse with anyone."**
Steve Brown

**"The learning never stops. Take each opportunity to be exposed to new ideas and skill sets. While it may not be directly relevant to today's challenges, it will often help for tomorrow's unexpected quiz."**
Mary Colleen Shanahan

**"Invest in your personal development. Have a unquenchable thirst for knowledge."**
Greg Shearson

When I graduated from business school, I carried the arrogance of many "biz school" grads. How could an arts student possibly function in business without having studied the lofty subjects of accounting, finance, marketing, and of course, HR?

Once again ... how wrong I was. A business degree is simply a door opener. My real business education started the day I walked into my "feeding pen" at Campbell Soup.

**"I understand the importance of my arts degree. Learning history helped me tremendously in marketing."**
Kevin O'Leary

As you embark on your career, keep in mind that your education is just beginning. Remember, your learning curve will be steep, endless, and exponential. Remember, a formal education, even a graduate degree, doesn't replace common sense.

Someone once advised me that "the problem with common sense is that it's just not that common."

**"A business degree is overrated. For the first several years of my marketing career, I was apologetic for not having a formal business education and was intimidated by those who did. Dave Thomas, founder of Wendy's and an early mentor, had a grade eight education. He taught me that the lack of formal education can readily be compensated for by a combination of common sense, a keen understanding of human nature, great listening skills, and of course, hard work."**
Jay Peters

If you lose your appetite for knowledge, and your thirst for new experiences and challenges, you—and your career—will atrophy. Don't be afraid of these. Embrace them.

**"Constant change is necessary not for the sake of it but because it keeps brands (and all things) relevant."**
Bill Moir

## KERNEL OF EXPERIENCE

The beginning of your career is the beginning of your education.

Your learning should never stop.

Be a sponge.

Be interested and interesting.

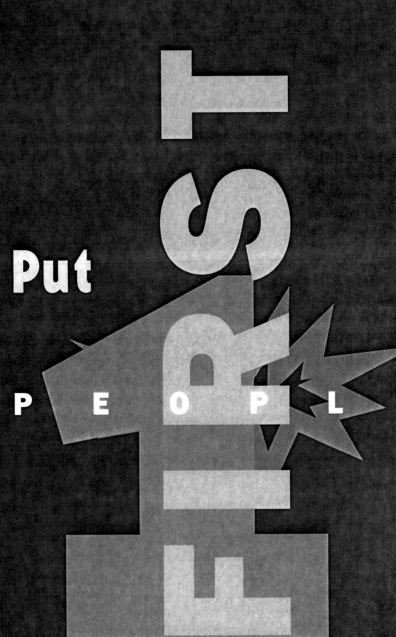

7

Put

FIRST

PEOPL

FIRST

**M**any of the lessons I acquired during my career were not from the people I reported to but from the people I worked with.

I remember a conversation I had with Susan Barclay, then an account director at Leo Burnett, Toronto. We were discussing the attributes of great leaders.

"They are those who are both liked and respected," she said. "They're the people you trust."

If people respect you but don't like you, they may do as you demand but will do so grudgingly. I worked with many clients and bosses whose intelligence and experience I admired and respected but whom I did not like.

One CEO I worked with was bright and accomplished, a nice enough person, but one who was interested only in his own ambitions, not the company's, and certainly not mine or others'. He was excellent at the functional part of his job but was not well liked.

He could get people to follow him but only reluctantly, out of fear or self-preservation. He was eventually ousted.

I know of a man who served a tour of duty in the army of his native Romania while it was still a Communist country, and then, after that, in the Israeli army.

The two experiences couldn't have been more different.

"In the Romanian army the officers put themselves first," he says. "They saw us as fodder for the cannons of their self-importance and authority. They would have been in grave danger if they had ever led us into war. Put a gun in our hands, and some of them wouldn't have made it out alive.

"In the Israeli army, the officers treated us as equals. They shared our living quarters and ate every meal with us, whether it was at camp or squatting down on the ground during maneuvers. We called them by their first names. We would have done anything for them."

At the same time, if a leader is simply liked and not respected, people may follow for a bit to be collegial but ultimately will think him a fool.

At one time, advertising agencies were filled with "hail fellows well met." They were long on socializing and interpersonal skills but short on hard work and smarts.

I once had reporting to me a regional account director our clients loved to socialize with. However, when it came to enlisting the agency's counsel, they sought out others. He was liked and not respected and in the end was fired.

No matter what career you choose, you will work with others and they will decide to follow your lead or not. If you're a one-person organization, you can do everything yourself. But go beyond that solo enterprise and you must rely on others. You've got to work for and with people, and you'll have to encourage others to follow you.

Susan Barclay was right: Great leaders are both liked and respected. Treat others as you would like to be treated, be empathetic, and approach issues from their points of views and they will follow you willingly.

Respect is earned, not demanded. You earn it by being honest. You earn it by being empathetic. You earn it by being courageous. You earn it by being responsible. You earn it by taking credit for the failures and sharing credit for the successes.

Ray Kroc, the founder of McDonald's, said, **"None of us is as good as all of us."**

**"There's very little you can do on your own. You need others' help. Seek out the best advice you can find and learn from it."**
Bob MacNelly

**"Winning teams are made of winners and as you begin to lead people your job will be much easier if you treat them so. Recognizing people's accomplishments goes a long way toward having them try harder and jump higher the next time. Try and make everyone a winner. Take some time to realize that looking good means making others look good. Spread the credit."**
Joe Hornick

**"Teams outperform individuals every time. Almost every company lists teamwork as one of its organizational values. But structuring your organization around high-performance, cross-functional teams is a very different concept—one that is surprisingly scarce in today's business world. I used to think hiring individuals with the most experience and the best track record was the right way to staff. I later learned it was far more productive to hire people with the right combination of complementary skills, personalities, and aptitude to win as a team."**
Jay Peters

People want to work with smart people, funny people, and optimistic people, people who are not afraid to show their vulnerabilities.

**"People like doing business with people they like. It took me quite a while to realize that this is a fundamental tenet of success. Be a relationship builder. Strive to know and care about the human being behind the business façade. Remember and ask about the personal details of your business associates' lives. Give of yourself. Show who you are as a person."**
Jim McKenzie

Late in my career I was introduced to Art Horn, an executive coach. Art has contributed to this book.

After about three coaching sessions, Art counseled me to be empathetic, to view the world from the perspectives of other people. Empathy wasn't my strong suit; it wasn't something that came naturally to me. It wasn't a management style that I had learned when working for autocratic companies early in my career.

I couldn't understand why if I thought something was a good idea everyone else didn't, too, and just follow my lead.

Wrong.

**"I wish I had understood the importance of empathy earlier in my career. The ability to frame your thinking with empathy yet still retain the integrity of your thoughts is an important lesson."**
Clive Sirkin

**"Always treat others the way you wish to be treated and life will be good or at least better."**
Pauleen Home

**"Treat your team like family. You probably spend more time with them, so it had better be a respectful and supportive environment for everyone."**
Ginny Dybenko

Perhaps not a lesson needed early in their careers but one many Boomers wish they had learned sooner is the importance of recruiting and retaining great people. Great people make great companies.

**"Always seek to hire the most outstanding candidates whose qualifications meet or exceed the requirements of the position."**
Charlie Scott

I learned the fine art of interviewing after making several mistakes and taking a management course in conducting professional interviews.

Often, panicked by a position that had been open too long and a client who was wondering why we couldn't recruit a quality candidate for their account, I chose poorly. I willed the next person into the job. They had a degree, had gone to the best school, had shiny shoes and a bright smile, so surely they'd be great.

Wrong again.

Having great people just makes life so much easier. The financial and emotional cost of firing and recruiting people is fatiguing. It's just not fun.

**"Surround yourself with A+ players."**
Ron Fabbro

**"You will always be successful if you understand and respect people who don't think the way you do."**
Keith Pelley

**"Surround yourself with good people. Don't be afraid of good people. Embrace them. You'll have a successor in the wings."**
Terry Jackson

**"Getting the right people is the most important decision you make. Never compromise. It nearly always backfires."**
John Clinton

**"Surround yourself with great people."**
Bernie Dyer

When you do make a hiring mistake, when you have hired someone who doesn't fit the culture, release them early.

My biggest regret in business was not dealing with the people who were technically good at their jobs but didn't fit our company culture. In one case, I knew I should have fired the person the day I met him. All my instincts—my "wee voice inside," as Leo Burnett called it—told me to get rid of him. I decided not to because he was good at generating revenue and passionate about advertising. He was not, however, passionate about his clients or his people. He was selfish and self-absorbed.

**"If a person does not fit the culture or meet the needs of job, deal with the problem early."**
Charlie Scott

## KERNEL OF
## EXPERIENCE

You can't do everything alone.

Recruit the best and the brightest and treat them the way you would like to be treated.

Work at having them both like and respect you.

Work at being trusted.

## 8

Be a Leader

I attended university with a fellow named John Stookes. He was an optimist and always full of infectious energy.

John played on the practice football team. This squad scrimmaged against the first stringers and were often referred to as the "hamburger squad" because they looked so beaten up at the end of every practice.

Undaunted and fueled by self-determination, John practiced hard every time.

He loathed indecision even if it was in deciding which pub to frequent, and this was often our most important decision. Frustrated by our collective indecisiveness, he would yell, "Be a leader."

It stuck with me. I can still hear him screaming it.

There is no such thing as a born leader. We learn to be leaders. We learn from those leaders we admire and those we don't.

There is no one type of leader. Look at Gandhi and Churchill, who battled each other over India's independence.

Churchill, one of history's great orators, led Britain with unbridled optimism, which buoyed his country's morale during some of its most difficult times, including the bombing of London during World War II.

Gandhi chose to lead through non-violent civil disobedience. His nationwide campaigns helped ease poverty, improve women's rights, and achieve independence for his country. He became a leader of leaders, with his methods eventually adopted by Martin Luther King, Jr., and Nelson Mandela.

I wish I had started learning to be a leader from my first day at work. I had been a high-school class captain; I had been a sports team captain. And I was born on August 21, which made me a Leo. Aren't all Leos natural-born leaders? I just assumed that I would lead and others would follow.

Wrong again.

Leadership is learned, and as in anything else, we learn to be leaders and the learning curve is exponential.

I learned to lead by trial and error, by observing others, by reading, by attending conferences, and by hiring a leadership coach. My leadership style evolved and hopefully improved with time and maturity.

The predominant leadership style I observed in the 1970s was autocratic, and this was the style I adopted early. Tell folks what to do and judge their performance based on how well they followed my orders. Empathy was for sissies.

This style worked in a recession when there were very few jobs, but as the economy improved, people had greater choice. Working for autocracies wasn't usually one of them.

With time, and mistakes, I learned to be more empathetic in my decisions. I'm not sure I ever got "all the way to bright," but if nothing else I was more aware.

In his book *Practice What You Preach*, David Maister offers several ideas on what it takes to lead. Successful leaders build supportive cultures. They:

- Act so everyone will succeed.

- Facilitate, don't dictate.

- Take work seriously, but don't take themselves seriously.

- Let people know they are a human being not just a leader.

- Create a casual, relaxed, collaborative environment but also a professional one.

- Show sensitivity to what people are going through.

Strong and effective leaders don't just lead those within their own organization; they also lead others. I learned as much if not more about leadership from some of my clients as from people in my own company.

**"Be the leader others choose to follow. There is no one leadership style or approach that works. When it comes your time to lead a small or a large group of people toward a common goal, the fact is it will be their choice whether they follow you or not. They will choose based not on your university degree, your style of dress, or how loudly you shout. They will choose based on whether you are taking them somewhere worthwhile; whether you can energize them to go there; whether you can help equip them for the journey; and whether you can muster the right support from others to make the journey successfully. They will also choose whether or not to follow you based on your character. They will evaluate your sincerity and your substance, and then they will decide to either follow you or not."**
Tim Penner

Learning to lead is different from learning to manage. Much of the executive training I took was focused on being a manager as opposed to being a leader. I wish someone had shown me how to inspire people as opposed to managing them.

"Managing isn't leading. Early in my career, I worked too hard and I'm sure I was too hard to work for. I was managing my job and the jobs of my direct reports as well. I was focused on what they were doing and how they were doing their jobs rather than on the results they were achieving. I was training employees to follow my orders and become overly dependent on my direction. I confused this micro-management with leadership. Later I learned that the essence of leadership is hiring people smarter than oneself and providing clear goals, the appropriate resources, the right rewards, and a good example to follow."

Jay Peters

## KERNEL OF
## EXPERIENCE

Leaders are not born.

Leaders learn to lead.

Learn to be someone others choose to follow.

Put your company and other people's interests before your own.

# 9

# Make
# Integrity
# Integral

**A**rt Horn, my leadership coach, once asked me this thought-provoking question: "What do you want your legacy to be?"

I'd never thought of it. I didn't think I was important enough to have a legacy.

How did I want to be remembered?

Upon reflection, I realized that I wanted to leave a legacy of trust. I wanted to be remembered for my integrity. (I have my parents and a smattering of Italian guilt to thank for that.)

My parents are people of honor. Their word is gospel. My father instilled in us the value of trust and to tell the truth at all costs. He drummed into us the fact that the consequences of lying are always far worse than those of telling the truth.

My mother was much the same. One must be brave to tell the truth, she told us. She taught us to be brave.

Every business is in the trust business, and we build trust by telling the truth.

When I worked in advertising, all I had to offer clients was my counsel. Nothing more. Nothing less. All I had to offer was the truth.

If I told a lie, even a tiny white lie, I'd lose their trust. And trust, once lost, is impossible to retrieve. You can't borrow it back. You can't buy it back. Trust's value cannot be monetized.

Lie and you're morally broke.

If I had lost a client's trust, I would have been out of business. If I had broken the trust bank, I would have been morally bankrupt.

You simply can't lie. One lie leads to another and another. You'll get caught. You'll be embarrassed and humiliated. You might get away with the first lie, even the second, but eventually you'll get caught.

Sure you can garner financial success by being dishonest, but you'll be ethically and morally broke. Success in life and business goes beyond your net worth.

Think about Enron, Tyco, and Hollinger. Fib, fib, fib...caught, caught, caught.

You will be tempted to fudge the truth, even if it's with your expense account.

I was lousy at submitting expenses. I always came up short. But I'd rather it cost me a few dollars than my reputation. I was tempted to fudge them, but I just couldn't.

87

I approved many expense accounts and most without incident. On those occasions when I found someone trying to bend the rules or claim expenses they hadn't incurred, it sickened me. Why would someone making a healthy six-figure income try to beat the company for the sake of $200?

Stephen Covey said, "You can't build trust without being trustworthy."

The folks who led Enron, Tyco, Hollinger, and other companies didn't build trust, because they weren't trustworthy.

**"Having a set of values that help guide you through the difficult decisions is one point that I would stress. If the groups you work with understand what you are about, how you go about making a decision, and how you will communicate it, then you have a much greater opportunity for the decision to be supported."**
Murray Ramsden

A clear conscience, doing the right thing, doing what you know should be done, is liberating. You'll lose enough sleep over work-related issues during your career. Don't exacerbate your insomnia by telling lies, skating around the truth, and rationalizing fibs.

Thankfully, I was never really challenged with the temptation to cheat at business. It just didn't occur to me.

One person who reported to me wanted to bury some costs against a client to cover for a mistake we had made. I was revolted. I should have fired him on the spot. I didn't, but I never trusted him again.

**"Integrity is the only thing. It's up to me and only me to take a stand when a potential action to be taken may seriously compromise my values. Doing what is unpopular, or even job threatening, in the name of 'what is right' is both freeing and empowering, and ultimately is the basis on which integrity is built or destroyed."**
Tom Collinger

Many people define themselves by what they do as opposed to who they are.

**"What you do for a living contributes to who you are, but it should never define who you are. Jobs will come and go. Careers will start and stop, but never lose sight of the things that truly define who you are: character, integrity, trust, honesty, humor, and loyalty."**
Tom Wright

If you were to write your retirement speech today, what would you say? If it's nothing other than that you strove to be a person of principle, that you wanted to be remembered for your integrity, that you didn't cheat, not even on your expenses, or lie, then you will have succeeded in business and in life.

Acting with integrity goes a long way toward ensuring that you will be comfortable in your own skin, knowing who you are and liking yourself.

**"Everybody should have a piece of paper in their files with the following question: 'Who am I?' Don't allow yourself to describe what you do or would like to do, but describe who you really are. Hard as it is, fiddle with this piece of paper once a year. When you have answered the question successfully, let yourself out of the cage. You are now free."**

Yong Quek

## KERNEL OF
## EXPERIENCE

- Build a legacy of trust.

- Always tell the truth.

- A clear conscience is liberating.

- Be a person of principle.

10

Give

BAC

**I** have given back, but not enough. I was the founding chairman of my wife's charity. I sat on the board of the Montreal YMCA. I coached hockey and was the president of the Evanston Youth Hockey organization. But I could have done more. It was often easier to write a check than to give of my time.

I feel so lucky to have lived the life I have lived, and I know I should do a better job of sharing my luck.

I first saw the power of giving back at age ten. My father was a Columbus Old Boy, having been a member of Columbus Boys Club, an inner city club, while growing up in Little Italy.

Every Christmas the Old Boys would deliver Toronto Star Christmas Boxes to needy families. Probably at my mother's prompting, Dad took me to deliver these boxes in 1960. We visited a poor single mom living in squalid conditions over a storefront, an elderly man living in a rooming house, and a family with what seemed to be an army of happy kids jammed into a small apartment.

The Christmas boxes were all they would receive at Christmas. They contained a scarf, a pair of woolen mittens, or some socks. That was it. No toys. No stockings hung from the fireplace, as there was neither a fireplace nor stockings.

My father may have taken me along for company only, but the life lesson stuck.

Someone once asked me in an interview if I felt lucky. I do; very much so. I have traveled the globe, lived in three great cities, played some of the world's finest golf courses, been married to the same woman for thirty-five years, been blessed with three sons I'm very proud of, am a member of a great golf club and sweaty old squash club, and can do what I want when I want and am still in good health.

I have been blessed with a great life, one that I take for granted all too often.

**"We are all blessed and have so many things our parents didn't have. They had only love and food to give and now our children have more toys in their bedrooms than my block had when I was growing up. If you are grateful each and every day, your life will grow."**
Hank Blank

Many of the people who have contributed to this book give of themselves and their money to their community, but two of them, Tim Penner and Terry Jackson, specifically mentioned giving back as a valuable lesson for those at the start of their careers.

I'm not surprised. Both are considered and considerate people. Both are bright, funny, and fair.

They give of their time as much as their money. It's easy to write a check. It's much more difficult to carve out some time from a busy schedule and give it.

**"Learn to give something back. If you do well in your career, then with that goes a responsibility to also do good. Give of your time and your money to help those less fortunate. Giving money is the easy part. Giving time is much more difficult, but it greatly enhances your learning and your character."**
Tim Penner

**"I feel strongly that it is an obligation for those of us who are blessed with good fortune or elevated position to use what we have to help others. We must give of our time, talent, and treasure. The joy of giving is returned many times over."**
Terry Jackson

Give back in any way you can.

**"Also remember that the smallest people in life can make you the largest. I gave a homeless woman in my neighborhood some money last week. She asked me if she could pray for me. I recognized that I was small and she was big because she wanted to help me with more than money."**
Hank Blank

My wife, Jo, relaunched her life by giving back. She created a charity in Toronto called Literature for Life that empowers at-risk teen moms through reading group circles, poetry writing, performance poetry, and the publication of two magazines. Jo has touched and influenced 3,500 young women since she started the charity eight years ago and has been recognized as a Woman of Distinction by the YWCA.

Some of the first people she helped are now graduating from college and university. By their own admission they couldn't have done it without her encouragement. When these young women speak of Jo, they do so with genuine love and affection.

Jo works tirelessly—at times through the night—for no other reason than to help others. She will tell you, as Terry does, that the joy of giving is returned many times over.

## KERNEL OF EXPERIENCE

Carve out some time for those less fortunate than you.

The joy of living will be returned several times over.

# Contributors

Jo Altilia
*Founder, Executive Director,*
Literature for Life

Tom Bene
*Senior Vice President of Sales,*
Pepsi-Cola, USA

Laurence Berstein
*Founder,*
BC3 Strategies

Hank Blank
*Founder,*
Hank Blank Inc.

Steve Brown
*Vice President, Advancement,*
Lawrence Technological University

Ted Clarke
*President,*
The Beer Store

John Clinton
*Senior Vice President and General Manager
of Consumer Publications,*
Transcontinental Media

Trevor Collier
*Founder,*
Trevor Collier Company

Tom Collinger
*Professor,*
Northwestern University

Mark Drexler
*Former General Manager,*
IBM Canada

Ginny Dybenko
*Dean, School of Business and Economics,*
Wilfrid Laurier University

Bernie Dyer
*President,*
East Side Mario's Restaurants

Bruce Elliott
*Past President,*
Labatt Breweries of Canada

Daryl Elliott
*Past Executive Vice President,*
*Director of Business Development,*
Y&R Advertising Worldwide

Ron Fabbro
*President and CEO,*
Specialty Catalog Corp.

John Farrow
*President,*
LEA International Ltd.

Henry Fiorillo
*Founder,*
RMG-Value Gap

Casey Forrest
*Prinicpal,*
Pinton Forrest & Madden

Robert Hall
*CEO,*
Ardale Enterprises

Doug Hayes
*Past President,*
Adidas Canada

Michael Hogg
*President,*
Hasbro Canada

Pauleen Home
*Past Practice Executive,*
IBM Global Services

Art Horn
*Founder,*
HORN

Joe Hornick
*Executive Director,*
Canadian Research Institute for
Law and the Family

Terry Jackson
*Past Executive Vice President,*
BMO Nesbitt Asset Management

Fred Jaques
*President,*
Santa Maria Foods

Eric Larson
*Chartered Accountant,*
Chicago

Michael MacMillan
*Founder,*
Alliance Atlantis

Bob MacNelly
*Executive Vice President, Marketing,*
Leon's Furniture

Tim McChesney
*Past Vice President, Marketing,*
Bell Canada

Jim McKenzie
*Past President,*
Leo Burnett, Canada

John McLean
*Past Principal,*
Mercer Consulting

Alan Middleton
*Executive Director,*
Schulich Executive Education Centre
*Assistant Professor of Marketing,*
York University

Bob Millar
*Past President and CEO,*
CKF Inc.

Bill Moir
*Executive Vice President, Marketing,*
Tim Hortons

Kevin O'Leary
*Vice President, Consulting,*
KWA Partners

David Ouchterlony
*Coroner and Palliative Care MD*
Toronto

Frank Palmer
*Chairman,*
DDB Group Canada

Keith Pelley
*President,*
CTV Olympic Consortium

Tim Penner
*President,*
Procter & Gamble, Canada

Jay Peters
*Corporate Director,*
Forzani Group Ltd.

Elizabeth Mast Priestman
*Managing Director,*
PGeSignature

Yong Quek
*Past President,*
Procter & Gamble, Canada

Murray Ramsden
*President and CEO,*
British Columbia Internal Health Authority

Charlie Scott
*Past President,*
Weston Bakeries

Mary Colleen Shanahan
*President,*
Tilley Endurables

Greg Shearson
*President and CEO,*
Jarden Outdoor Solutions

Clive Sirkin
*Former Group Managing Director,*
Leo Burnett Worldwide

Tom Wright
*Past Commissioner,*
Canadian Football League

# About the Author

**Tony Altilia** retired from corporate life at 57 after working for over thirty years for multinational advertising agencies in Canada and the United States. He retired as the President/CEO of DDB's Downtown Partners, one of Canada's most highly awarded agencies.

A graduate of Wilfrid Laurier's business school, Tony started his career in brand management at the Campbell Soup Company and later helped champion brands Procter and Gamble, Kraft, Pepsi, McDonald's, Reebok, and others.

A father of three Millennial sons, Tony now spends his time teaching brands at the Ontario College of Art and Design and running a brand consultancy along with his partner Jim McKenzie.

CPSIA information can be obtained at www.ICGtesting.com
Printed in the USA
LVOW10s0543300116

472771LV00014B/47/P